The Family Register

of Personal and Financial Papers

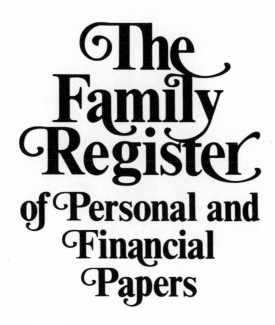

The Family Register

of Personal and Financial Papers

U.S.NEWS & WORLD REPORT BOOKS

A division of U.S.News & World Report, Inc.
WASHINGTON, D.C.

Book Trade Distribution by Simon and Schuster
Simon and Schuster Order Number 22127

ISBN 0-89193-418-9

Library of Congress Catalog Card Number 75-13697

Printed in the United States of America

CONTENTS

Part One: Important Papers
Family Members / 9
Medical Data / 10
Financial and Personal Counselors / 12
Bank Accounts / 14
Safe Deposit Boxes / 14
Location of Documents / 15

Part Two: Property
Real Estate / 19
Automobiles / 23
Motorcycle / 26
Boat / 26

Part Three: Investments
Stocks / 29
Mutual Funds / 32
Municipal and Industrial Bonds / 33
Government Bonds / 35
Other Investments / 37

Part Four: Insurance
Life Insurance / 41
Cash-Value and Paid-Up Life Insurance / 42
Health and Accident Insurance / 43
Property Insurance / 44
Automobile Insurance / 48

**Part Five: Employment and Self-
            Employment Benefits**
Pension/Annuity / 53
Profit Sharing / 55
Individual Retirement Account / 57
Keogh Plan / 59

Part Six: Financial Records
Balance Sheet / 63
Income Record / 66
Tax-Deductible Expenditures / 69
Loans (Payments Due Others) / 72
Loans (Payments Receivable) / 73
Credit Cards and Charge Accounts / 74

Part Seven: Household Operations
Monthly Operating Budget / 77
Monthly Expense Reminder / 80
Utility Expenses / 86
Automobile Expenditures / 87
Home Improvements / 90
Home Repairs / 91
Appliance Service Record / 92

Part Eight: Household Inventory
Room-by-Room / 95
Other Articles / 113
Summary of Inventory / 124

Part One   **IMPORTANT PAPERS**

Family Members

Medical Data

Financial and Personal Counselors

Bank Accounts

Safe Deposit Boxes

Location of Documents

IMPORTANT PAPERS

Family Members

Name	Date of Birth	Address	Telephone

IMPORTANT PAPERS

Medical Data

Family Member	Blood Type	Type and Date of Inoculation	Type and Date of Injury or Disease

IMPORTANT PAPERS

**Family Doctors, Dentists,
and Specialists**

Doctor	Address	Telephone

IMPORTANT PAPERS

**Family Financial
and Personal Counselors**

Adviser	Firm and Address	Telephone
Accountants		
Attorneys		
Bankers		
Business Partners		
Clergymen		
Executors of Will		

IMPORTANT PAPERS

**Family Financial
and Personal Counselors**

Adviser	Firm and Address	Telephone
Insurance Agents		
Tax Consultants		
Trust Officers		
Other		

IMPORTANT PAPERS

Bank Accounts

Bank	Address	Account in the Name of	Account Number	Location of Passbook

Safe Deposit Boxes

Bank	Address	Box in the Name of	Number	Location of Key	Who Has Access

IMPORTANT PAPERS

Location of Documents

Papers	Location
Certificates: Marriage	
Birth	
Baptismal	
Securities	
Wills: Head of Household (original)	
Copies	
Other Family Members:	
Military Service Records	
Social Security Cards and Numbers	
Employment Records	
Automobile Title and Registration	
Education Records (Expenses and Transcripts)	
Medical and Health Records	
Insurance Policies	
Adoption Papers	
Divorce or Separation Papers	
Passports	
Citizenship Papers	
Income Tax Returns	
Other Tax Records	
Other	

IMPORTANT PAPERS

Location of Documents

Papers	Location

Part Two   **PROPERTY**

Real Estate

Automobiles

Motorcycle

Boat

PROPERTY

Real Estate

☐ Residence
☐ Summer
☐ Investment

Address   Lot No.   Block No.

Title in the name of   Title insurance policy No.

Title company   Address

Recorded in: City   County   State

Date recorded   Deed book No.   Page No.

Previous owner   Date purchased

Purchase price   Cash paid   Balance

Mortgage Information

First mortgage: Mortgagee

Mortgagor

Date recorded   No. of years   Loan No.

Amount of mortgage   % interest

When payments are due   Amount

Second mortgage: Mortgagee

Mortgagor

Date recorded   No. of years   Loan No.

Amount of mortgage   % interest

When payments are due   Amount

Assessed tax value: 19___ Amount   19___ Amount

19___ Amount   19___ Amount

PROPERTY

Real Estate

☐ Residence
☐ Summer
☐ Investment

Address	Lot No.	Block No.
Title in the name of	Title insurance policy No.	
Title company	Address	
Recorded in: City	County	State
Date recorded	Deed book No.	Page No.
Previous owner	Date purchased	
Purchase price	Cash paid	Balance

Mortgage Information

First mortgage: Mortgagee

Mortgagor

Date recorded	No. of years	Loan No.
Amount of mortgage	% interest	
When payments are due	Amount	

Second mortgage: Mortgagee

Mortgagor

Date recorded	No. of years	Loan No.
Amount of mortgage	% interest	
When payments are due	Amount	
Assessed tax value: 19____ Amount	19____ Amount	
19____ Amount	19____ Amount	

PROPERTY

Real Estate

☐ Residence
☐ Summer
☐ Investment

Address	Lot No.	Block No.
Title in the name of	Title insurance policy No.	
Title company	Address	
Recorded in: City	County	State
Date recorded	Deed book No.	Page No.
Previous owner		Date purchased
Purchase price	Cash paid	Balance

Mortgage Information

First mortgage: Mortgagee

Mortgagor

Date recorded	No. of years	Loan No.
Amount of mortgage	% interest	
When payments are due	Amount	

Second mortgage: Mortgagee

Mortgagor

Date recorded	No. of years	Loan No.
Amount of mortgage	% interest	
When payments are due	Amount	

Assessed tax value: 19___ Amount   19___ Amount

19___ Amount   19___ Amount

PROPERTY

Real Estate

☐ Residence
☐ Summer
☐ Investment

Address	Lot No.	Block No.
Title in the name of	Title insurance policy No.	
Title company	Address	
Recorded in: City	County	State
Date recorded	Deed book No.	Page No.
Previous owner	Date purchased	
Purchase price	Cash paid	Balance

Mortgage Information

First mortgage: Mortgagee		
Mortgagor		
Date recorded	No. of years	Loan No.
Amount of mortgage	% interest	
When payments are due	Amount	
Second mortgage: Mortgagee		
Mortgagor		
Date recorded	No. of years	Loan No.
Amount of mortgage	% interest	
When payments are due	Amount	
Assessed tax value: 19___ Amount	19___ Amount	
19___ Amount	19___ Amount	

PROPERTY

Automobile

Title in the name of

Location of title

Make   Year

Model   Color

Serial No.   Engine type, size, and No.

Ignition key No.   Trunk key No.

Identifiable marks

Dealer   Salesman

Address

Purchase price   Warranty period

Location of service receipts

Bank or lender

Amount of loan   % interest   Date of loan

No. of loan   Number of payments

When due   Monthly payment

PROPERTY

Automobile

Title in the name of

Location of title

Make   Year

Model   Color

Serial No.   Engine type, size, and No.

Ignition key No.   Trunk key No.

Identifiable marks

Dealer   Salesman

Address

Purchase price   Warranty period

Location of service receipts

Bank or lender

Amount of loan   % interest   Date of loan

No. of loan   Number of payments

When due   Monthly payment

PROPERTY

Automobile

Title in the name of

Location of title

Make   Year

Model   Color

Serial No.   Engine type, size, and No.

Ignition key No.   Trunk key No.

Identifiable marks

Dealer   Salesman

Address

Purchase price   Warranty period

Location of service receipts

Bank or lender

Amount of loan   % interest   Date of loan

No. of loan   Number of payments

When due   Monthly payment

PROPERTY

Motorcycle

Title in the name of

Location of title

Make   Year

Model   Color

Serial No.   Engine type, size, and No.

Identifiable marks

Dealer   Salesman

Address

Purchase price   Warranty period

Location of service receipts

Boat

Title in the name of

Location of title

Make   Year

Model   Color

Serial No.   Engine type, size, and No.

Identifiable marks

Dealer   Salesman

Address

Purchase price   Warranty period

Location of service receipts

Bank or lender

Amount of loan   % interest   Date of loan

No. of loan   Number of payments

When due   Monthly payment

Part Three **INVESTMENTS**

Stocks

Mutual Funds

Municipal and Industrial Bonds

Government Bonds

Other Investments

INVESTMENTS

Stocks

Company	No. of Shares	Price per Share	Purchase Date	Certificate No.	Owner(s)	Shares Sold		
						No. of Shares	Date	Gain or Loss

INVESTMENTS

Stocks

Company	No. of Shares	Price per Share	Purchase Date	Certificate No.	Owner(s)	Shares Sold		
						No. of Shares	Date	Gain or Loss

INVESTMENTS

Stocks

Company	No. of Shares	Price per Share	Purchase Date	Certificate No.	Owner(s)	Shares Sold		
						No. of Shares	Date	Gain or Loss

INVESTMENTS
Mutual Funds

Fund	No. of Shares	Price per Share	Purchase Date	Certificate No.	Owner(s)	Shares Sold		
						No. of Shares	Date	Gain or Loss

INVESTMENTS

Municipal and Industrial Bonds

Municipality or Company	No. of Units	Price per Unit	Purchase Date	Serial No.	Face Value	Owner(s)	% Interest	Maturity Date	Sold		
									Serial No.	Date	Price

INVESTMENTS

Municipal and Industrial Bonds

Municipality or Company	No. of Units	Price per Unit	Purchase Date	Serial No.	Face Value	Owner(s)	% Interest	Maturity Date	Serial No.	Sold Date	Price

INVESTMENTS

Government Bonds

Series No.	No. of Units	Price per Unit	Purchase Date	Face Value	Interest Rate	Owner(s)	Maturity Date	Surrender Value	Accrued Interest

INVESTMENTS

Government Bonds

Series No.	No. of Units	Price per Unit	Purchase Date	Face Value	Interest Rate	Owner(s)	Maturity Date	Surrender Value	Accrued Interest

INVESTMENTS
Other Investments

Name of Business	Type of Business	Address and Phone	Date Invested	Amount Invested	% Ownership	Other Owner(s)

INVESTMENTS

Other Investments

Name of Business	Type of Business	Address and Phone	Date Invested	Amount Invested	% Ownership	Other Owner(s)

Part Four   **INSURANCE**

Life Insurance

**Summary of Cash Value and
Paid-Up Life Insurance**

Health and Accident Insurance

Property Insurance

Automobile Insurance

INSURANCE

Life Insurance

Name of Insured	Policy Owner	Company	Policy No.	Face Value	Date Issued	Premium	Date Due	Beneficiary(s)

INSURANCE

Summary of Cash Value
and
Paid-Up Life Insurance

Year	Policy No.	Company	Cash Value	Paid-Up Insurance

INSURANCE

Health and Accident Insurance

Name of Insured	Policy Owner	Company	Policy No.	Type Coverage	Date Issued	Premium	Date Due	Policy Expires

INSURANCE

Property Insurance

Name of insured

Company _____ Agent

Address _____ Phone

Type of policy

Description of insured property

Location of property

Policy No. _____ Date issued _____ Date expires

Face Value $ _____ Amount deductible $

Annual premium $ _____ Date due

Location of Policy

Coverage	Liability Limit	Premium Rate per $1,000
Homeowners ☐ Basic ☐ Broad ☐ Comprehensive		
Fire or lightning		
Smoke		
Theft		
Burglary or vandalism		
Explosion		
Water damage		
Glass breakage		
Bodily injury (medical)		
Loss of property		
Other		

INSURANCE

Property Insurance

Name of insured

Company   Agent

Address   Phone

Type of policy

Description of insured property

Location of property

Policy No.   Date issued   Date expires

Face Value $ Amount deductible $

Annual premium $ Date due

Location of Policy

Coverage	Liability Limit	Premium Rate per $1,000
Homeowners ☐ Basic ☐ Broad ☐ Comprehensive		
Fire or lightning		
Smoke		
Theft		
Burglary or vandalism		
Explosion		
Water damage		
Glass breakage		
Bodily injury (medical)		
Loss of property		
Other		

INSURANCE

Property Insurance

Name of insured

Company   Agent

Address   Phone

Type of policy

Description of insured property

Location of property

Policy No.   Date issued   Date expires

Face Value $ Amount deductible $

Annual premium $ Date due

Location of Policy

Coverage	Liability Limit	Premium Rate per $1,000
Homeowners ☐ Basic ☐ Broad ☐ Comprehensive		
Fire or lightning		
Smoke		
Theft		
Burglary or vandalism		
Explosion		
Water damage		
Glass breakage		
Bodily injury (medical)		
Loss of property		
Other		

INSURANCE

<table>
<tr><td colspan="3" align="center">

Property Insurance

</td></tr>
<tr><td colspan="3">Name of insured</td></tr>
<tr><td colspan="2">Company</td><td>Agent</td></tr>
<tr><td colspan="2">Address</td><td>Phone</td></tr>
<tr><td colspan="3">Type of policy</td></tr>
<tr><td colspan="3">Description of insured property</td></tr>
<tr><td colspan="3"></td></tr>
<tr><td colspan="3">Location of property</td></tr>
<tr><td>Policy No.</td><td>Date issued</td><td>Date expires</td></tr>
<tr><td>Face Value $</td><td colspan="2">Amount deductible $</td></tr>
<tr><td>Annual premium $</td><td colspan="2">Date due</td></tr>
<tr><td colspan="3">Location of Policy</td></tr>
</table>

Coverage	Liability Limit	Premium Rate per $1,000
Homeowners ☐ Basic ☐ Broad ☐ Comprehensive		
Fire or lightning		
Smoke		
Theft		
Burglary or vandalism		
Explosion		
Water damage		
Glass breakage		
Bodily injury (medical)		
Loss of property		
Other		

INSURANCE

Automobile Insurance

Make	Year
Model	Name of insured
Company	Agent
Address	Phone
Policy No.	
Date issued	Date expires
Annual premium	Date due

Coverage	Liability Limit	Premium Rate per $1,000
Comprehensive		
Bodily injury		
Medical		
Collision		
Uninsured motorist		
Property damage		
Other		

INSURANCE

Automobile Insurance

Make		Year
Model	Name of insured	
Company		Agent
Address		Phone
Policy No.		
Date issued	Date expires	
Annual premium	Date due	

Coverage	Liability Limit	Premium Rate per $1,000
Comprehensive		
Bodily injury		
Medical		
Collision		
Uninsured motorist		
Property damage		
Other		

INSURANCE

Automobile Insurance		
Make		Year
Model	Name of insured	
Company		Agent
Address		Phone
Policy No.		
Date issued	Date expires	
Annual premium	Date due	

Coverage	Liability Limit	Premium Rate per $1,000
Comprehensive		
Bodily injury		
Medical		
Collision		
Uninsured motorist		
Property damage		
Other		

Part Five

EMPLOYMENT AND
SELF-EMPLOYMENT BENEFITS

Pension/Annuity

Profit Sharing

Individual Retirement Account

Keogh Plan

EMPLOYMENT BENEFITS

☐ **Pension** or ☐ **Annuity**

Plan in whose name

Beneficiary   Address

Contingent beneficiary   Address

Employer   Address

Trustee(s)   Person to contact

Insurance company

Type of plan

If employee contributes: yearly   % $

Employer contributes: yearly   % $

Initial contribution date

Eligibility date   Age

Retirement date   Age

Vesting schedule   %   Year

Disability benefits $

Insurance death benefit $ Retirement benefits $

Number of years certain   Payable life income $

Other benefits or provisions:

EMPLOYMENT BENEFITS

□ **Pension or** □ **Annuity**

Plan in whose name

Beneficiary   Address

Contingent beneficiary   Address

Employer   Address

Trustee(s)   Person to contact

Insurance company

Type of plan

If employee contributes: yearly   % $

Employer contributes: yearly   % $

Initial contribution date

Eligibility date   Age

Retirement date   Age

Vesting schedule   %   Year

Disability benefits $

Insurance death benefit $ Retirement benefits $

Number of years certain   Payable life income $

Other benefits or provisions:

EMPLOYMENT BENEFITS

Profit Sharing

Plan in whose name

Name of plan

Beneficiary   Address

Contingent beneficiary   Address

Employer   Address

Trustee(s)   Person to contact

Eligibility date   Retirement date

If employee contributes: yearly $

Benefits

Restrictions

Transactions

Date	No. of Shares Added	Value	Cumulative Value

EMPLOYMENT BENEFITS

Profit Sharing

Plan in whose name

Name of plan

Beneficiary   Address

Contingent beneficiary   Address

Employer   Address

Trustee(s)   Person to contact

Eligibility date   Retirement date

If employee contributes: yearly $

Benefits

Restrictions

Transactions

Date	No. of Shares Added	Value	Cumulative Value

EMPLOYMENT BENEFITS

Individual Retirement Account

Date	Amount Invested	Total Value

EMPLOYMENT BENEFITS

Individual Retirement Account

Date	Amount Invested	Total Value

EMPLOYMENT BENEFITS

SELF-EMPLOYMENT BENEFITS

Keogh Plan

Date	Amount Invested	Total Value

SELF-EMPLOYMENT BENEFITS

Keogh Plan

Date	Amount Invested	Total Value

Part Six   **FINANCIAL RECORDS**

Balance Sheet

Income Records

Tax-Deductible Expenditures

Loans (Payments Due Others)

Loans (Payments Receivable)

Credit Cards and Charge Accounts

FINANCIAL RECORDS

Balance Sheet
as of _____
Date

Assets	Liabilities
Real Estate	Mortgages
Personal Property	Taxes
Autos	Operating Expenses
Business Accounts Receivable	Business Accounts Payable
Cash	Insurance Premiums
Savings	Loans (Payments Due Others)
Checking	Installments
Time Deposits	Charge Accounts
Stocks	Other Liabilities
Mutual Funds	
Bonds	
Government Bonds	
Pension	
Annuity	
Profit-Sharing	
Cash-Value Life Insurance	
Loans (Payments Receivable)	
Other Assets	
Total Assets	Total Liabilities
	Total Assets
	Less Total Liabilities
	Net Worth

FINANCIAL RECORDS

Balance Sheet
as of _____
Date

Assets	Liabilities
Real Estate	Mortgages
Personal Property	Taxes
Autos	Operating Expenses
Business Accounts Receivable	Business Accounts Payable
Cash	Insurance Premiums
Savings	Loans (Payments Due Others)
Checking	Installments
Time Deposits	Charge Accounts
Stocks	Other Liabilities
Mutual Funds	
Bonds	
Government Bonds	
Pension	
Annuity	
Profit-Sharing	
Cash-Value Life Insurance	
Loans (Payments Receivable)	
Other Assets	
Total Assets	Total Liabilities
	Total Assets
	Less Total Liabilities
	Net Worth

FINANCIAL RECORDS

Balance Sheet
as of _____
Date

Assets	Liabilities
Real Estate	Mortgages
Personal Property	Taxes
Autos	Operating Expenses
Business Accounts Receivable	Business Accounts Payable
Cash	Insurance Premiums
Savings	Loans (Payments Due Others)
Checking	Installments
Time Deposits	Charge Accounts
Stocks	Other Liabilities
Mutual Funds	
Bonds	
Government Bonds	
Pension	
Annuity	
Profit-Sharing	
Cash-Value Life Insurance	
Loans (Payments Receivable)	
Other Assets	
Total Assets	Total Liabilities
	Total Assets
	Less Total Liabilities
	Net Worth

FINANCIAL RECORDS

Income Record

for 19_____

Date	Source of Income	Amount of Salary or Commission	Bank Interest	Returns on Stocks/Bonds	Other	T-Taxable N-Nontaxable

FINANCIAL RECORDS

Income Record

for 19_____

Date	Source of Income	Amount of Salary or Commission	Bank Interest	Returns on Stocks/Bonds	Other	T-Taxable N-Nontaxable

FINANCIAL RECORDS

Income Record

for 19_____.

Date	Source of Income	Amount of Salary or Commission	Bank Interest	Returns on Stocks/Bonds	Other	T-Taxable N-Nontaxable

FINANCIAL RECORDS

Tax-Deductible Expenditures
for 19_____

Date	To Whom Paid	Business	Charity	Interest	Taxes	Other

FINANCIAL RECORDS

Tax-Deductible Expenditures
for 19_____

Date	To Whom Paid	Business	Charity	Interest	Taxes	Other

FINANCIAL RECORDS

Tax-Deductible Expenditures
for 19_____

Date	To Whom Paid	Business	Charity	Interest	Taxes	Other

FINANCIAL RECORDS

Loans (Payments Due Others)

Amount		To Whom Paid	Purpose	Date Borrowed	Repayment Plan	Final Payment Due
Principal	Interest					

FINANCIAL RECORDS

Loans (Payments Receivable)

Amount		From Whom Received	Purpose	Date Borrowed	Repayment Plan	Final Payment Due
Principal	Interest					

FINANCIAL RECORDS

Credit Cards and Charge Accounts

Name of Company	Account No.	Authorized Signature(s)	Date Expires

Part Seven

HOUSEHOLD OPERATIONS

Monthly Operating Budget

Monthly Expense Reminder

Utility Expenses

Automobile Expenditures

Home Improvements

Home Repairs

Appliance Service Record

Monthly Operating Budget for 19____

		Jan.	Feb.	March	April	May	June	July	Aug.	Sept.	Oct.	Nov.	Dec.	Total
	Total Income													
Fixed Payments	Mortgage (rent)													
	Taxes													
	Insurance													
	Loans (Payments due to others)													
	Savings													
	Total Fixed Payments													
Flexible Payments	Utilities													
	House Improvements/Repairs													
	Food													
	Clothing													
	Medical/Dental													
	Education													
	Recreation													
	Magazines/Newspapers													
	Contributions													
	Automobile Expenditures													
	Credit Charges													
	Other													
	Total Flexible Payments													
Budget	Total Fixed and Flexible													
	Total Income													
	Balance (+ or −)													

HOUSEHOLD OPERATIONS

Monthly Operating Budget for 19_____

		Jan.	Feb.	March	April	May	June	July	Aug.	Sept.	Oct.	Nov.	Dec.	Total
	Total Income													
Fixed Payments	Mortgage (rent)													
	Taxes													
	Insurance													
	Loans (Payments due to others)													
	Savings													
	Total Fixed Payments													
Flexible Payments	Utilities													
	House Improvements/Repairs													
	Food													
	Clothing													
	Medical/Dental													
	Education													
	Recreation													
	Magazines/Newspapers													
	Contributions													
	Automobile Expenditures													
	Credit Charges													
	Other													
	Total Flexible Payments													
Budget	Total Fixed and Flexible													
	Total Income													
	Balance (+ or −)													

HOUSEHOLD OPERATIONS

Monthly Operating Budget for 19_____

		Jan.	Feb.	March	April	May	June	July	Aug.	Sept.	Oct.	Nov.	Dec.	Total
	Total Income													
Fixed Payments	Mortgage (rent)													
	Taxes													
	Insurance													
	Loans (Payments due to others)													
	Savings													
	Total Fixed Payments													
Flexible Payments	Utilities													
	House Improvements/Repairs													
	Food													
	Clothing													
	Medical/Dental													
	Education													
	Recreation													
	Magazines/Newspapers													
	Contributions													
	Automobile Expenditures													
	Credit Charges													
	Other													
	Total Flexible Payments													
Budget	Total Fixed and Flexible													
	Total Income													
	Balance (+ or −)													

HOUSEHOLD OPERATIONS

Monthly Expense Reminder for 19____

Fixed payments due during the year, such as mortgage, rent, insurance premiums, loans, school tuition.

Expense	January		February		March		April		May		June		Total
	Day Due	Amount	Day Due	Amount	Day Due	Amount	Day Due	Amount	Day Due	Amount	Day Due	Amount	
Total													

HOUSEHOLD OPERATIONS

Monthly Expense Reminder for 19___

Fixed payments due during the year, such as mortgage, rent, insurance premiums, loans, school tuition.

Expense	July		August		September		October		November		December		Total
	Day Due	Amount	Day Due	Amount	Day Due	Amount	Day Due	Amount	Day Due	Amount	Day Due	Amount	
Total													

HOUSEHOLD OPERATIONS

Monthly Expense Reminder for 19____

Fixed payments due during the year, such as mortgage, rent, insurance premiums, loans, school tuition.

Expense	January		February		March		April		May		June		Total
	Day Due	Amount	Day Due	Amount	Day Due	Amount	Day Due	Amount	Day Due	Amount	Day Due	Amount	
Total													

HOUSEHOLD OPERATIONS

Monthly Expense Reminder for 19____

Fixed payments due during the year, such as mortgage, rent, insurance premiums, loans, school tuition.

Expense	July		August		September		October		November		December		Total
	Day Due	Amount	Day Due	Amount	Day Due	Amount	Day Due	Amount	Day Due	Amount	Day Due	Amount	
Total													

HOUSEHOLD OPERATIONS

Monthly Expense Reminder for 19____

Fixed payments due during the year, such as mortgage, rent, insurance premiums, loans, school tuition.

Expense	January		February		March		April		May		June		Total
	Day Due	Amount	Day Due	Amount	Day Due	Amount	Day Due	Amount	Day Due	Amount	Day Due	Amount	
Total													

HOUSEHOLD OPERATIONS

Monthly Expense Reminder for 19____

Fixed payments due during the year, such as mortgage, rent, insurance premiums, loans, school tuition.

Expense	July		August		September		October		November		December		Total
	Day Due	Amount	Day Due	Amount	Day Due	Amount	Day Due	Amount	Day Due	Amount	Day Due	Amount	
Total													

HOUSEHOLD OPERATIONS

Utility Expenses

19_____	Jan.	Feb.	March	April	May	June	July	Aug.	Sept.	Oct.	Nov.	Dec.	Total
Electric													
Gas													
Heat													
Water													
Phone													
Other													
Total													

19_____	Jan.	Feb.	March	April	May	June	July	Aug.	Sept.	Oct.	Nov.	Dec.	Total
Electric													
Gas													
Heat													
Water													
Phone													
Other													
Total													

19_____	Jan.	Feb.	March	April	May	June	July	Aug.	Sept.	Oct.	Nov.	Dec.	Total
Electric													
Gas													
Heat													
Water													
Phone													
Other													
Total													

HOUSEHOLD OPERATIONS

Automobile Expenditures

Car_____   19_____

	Jan.	Feb.	March	April	May	June	July	Aug.	Sept.	Oct.	Nov.	Dec.	Total
Gas													
Oil													
Tires													
Battery													
Tune-ups													
Accessories													
Parking Costs													
License Fees													
Inspection													
Insurance													
Repairs													
Other													
Total Costs													
Total Mileage													
Cost per Mile													

HOUSEHOLD OPERATIONS

Automobile Expenditures

Car_____   19_____

	Jan.	Feb.	March	April	May	June	July	Aug.	Sept.	Oct.	Nov.	Dec.	Total
Gas													
Oil													
Tires													
Battery													
Tune-ups													
Accessories													
Parking Costs													
License Fees													
Inspection													
Insurance													
Repairs													
Other													
Total Costs													
Total Mileage													
Cost per Mile													

HOUSEHOLD OPERATIONS

Automobile Expenditures

Car_____   19_____

	Jan.	Feb.	March	April	May	June	July	Aug.	Sept.	Oct.	Nov.	Dec.	Total
Gas													
Oil													
Tires													
Battery													
Tune-ups													
Accessories													
Parking Costs													
License Fees													
Inspection													
Insurance													
Repairs													
Other													
Total Costs													
Total Mileage													
Cost per Mile													

Home Improvements

Capital Improvement	Date	By Whom	Cost

HOUSEHOLD OPERATIONS

Home Repairs

Repair	Date	By Whom	Cost

HOUSEHOLD OPERATIONS

Appliance Service Record

Item	Service	Date	By Whom	Cost

Entrance Hall

Den/Family Room

Library

Living Room

Dining Room

Kitchen/Breakfast Area

Bedrooms

Bathrooms

Linen and Storage Closets

Utility Room

Attic

Basement

Garage

China

Silver

Appliances

Books

Musical Instruments

Photographic Equipment

Coins

Stamps

Jewelry

Furs

Property Not Listed Elsewhere

Summary of Household Inventory

HOUSEHOLD INVENTORY

Entrance Hall

Article	Description	Purchase Date	Original Price	Insured Value
Carpeting				
Rugs				
Drapery				
Shades				
Light fixtures				
Tables				
Chairs				
Mirrors				
Lamps				
Art				
Other				

HOUSEHOLD INVENTORY

Den/Family Room

Article	Description	Purchase Date	Original Price	Insured Value
Carpeting				
Rugs				
Drapery				
Shades				
Light fixtures				
Tables				
Chairs				
Sofas				
Desk				
Lamps				
Bookcases				
Art				
Other				

HOUSEHOLD INVENTORY

Library

Article	Description	Purchase Date	Original Price	Insured Value
Carpeting				
Rugs				
Drapery				
Shades				
Light fixtures				
Tables				
Chairs				
Sofas				
Desk				
Bookcases				
Art				
Other*				

HOUSEHOLD INVENTORY

Living Room

Article	Description	Purchase Date	Original Price	Insured Value
Carpeting				
Rugs				
Drapery				
Shades				
Light fixtures				
Tables				
Chairs				
Sofas				
Bookcases				
Art				
Other				

HOUSEHOLD INVENTORY

Dining Room

Article	Description	Purchase Date	Original Price	Insured Value
Carpeting				
Rugs				
Drapery				
Shades				
Lighting fixtures				
Tables				
Chairs				
Buffet				
China cabinet				
Cupboard				
Art				
Other				

HOUSEHOLD INVENTORY

Kitchen/Breakfast Area

Article	Description	Purchase Date	Original Price	Insured Value
Flooring				
Curtains				
Shades				
Lighting fixtures				
Tables				
Chairs				
Cabinets				
Flatware				
Dishes				
Glassware				
Cooking utensils				
Other*				

*For appliances, see page 114.

HOUSEHOLD INVENTORY

Bedroom

Article	Description	Purchase Date	Original Price	Insured Value
Carpeting				
Rugs				
Drapery				
Shades				
Lighting fixtures				
Bureaus				
Chests of drawers				
Beds				
Bedding				
Nightstands				
Dressing table				
Chairs				
Desk				
Other				

HOUSEHOLD INVENTORY

Bedroom

Article	Description	Purchase Date	Original Price	Insured Value
Carpeting				
Rugs				
Drapery				
Shades				
Lighting fixtures				
Bureaus				
Chests of drawers				
Beds				
Bedding				
Nightstands				
Dressing table				
Chairs				
Desk				
Other				

HOUSEHOLD INVENTORY

Bedroom

Article	Description	Purchase Date	Original Price	Insured Value
Carpeting				
Rugs				
Drapery				
Shades				
Lighting fixtures				
Bureaus				
Chests of drawers				
Beds				
Bedding				
Nightstands				
Dressing table				
Chairs				
Desk				
Other				

HOUSEHOLD INVENTORY

Bedroom

Article	Description	Purchase Date	Original Price	Insured Value
Carpeting				
Rugs				
Drapery				
Shades				
Lighting fixtures				
Bureaus				
Chests of drawers				
Beds				
Bedding				
Nightstands				
Dressing table				
Chairs				
Desk				
Other				

HOUSEHOLD INVENTORY

Bathroom

Article	Description	Purchase Date	Original Price	Insured Value
Carpeting				
Rugs				
Shades				
Lighting fixtures				
Cabinets				
Shelving				
Mirrors				
Hamper				
Other				

HOUSEHOLD INVENTORY

Bathroom

Article	Description	Purchase Date	Original Price	Insured Value
Carpeting				
Rugs				
Shades				
Lighting fixtures				
Cabinets				
Shelving				
Mirrors				
Hamper				
Other				

HOUSEHOLD INVENTORY

Bathroom

Article	Description	Purchase Date	Original Price	Insured Value
Carpeting				
Rugs				
Shades				
Lighting fixtures				
Cabinets				
Shelving				
Mirrors				
Hamper				
Other				

HOUSEHOLD INVENTORY

Linen and Storage Closets

Article and Location	Purchase Date	Original Price	Insured Value

HOUSEHOLD INVENTORY

Utility Room

Article	Description	Purchase Date	Original Price	Insured Value
Flooring				
Cabinets				
Other*				

HOUSEHOLD INVENTORY

Attic

Article	Description	Purchase Date	Original Price	Insured Value

HOUSEHOLD INVENTORY

	Basement			
Article	Description	Purchase Date	Original Price	Insured Value

HOUSEHOLD INVENTORY

Garage

Article	Description	Purchase Date	Original Price	Insured Value

HOUSEHOLD INVENTORY

China

Description of Article and Location	Purchase Date	Original Price	Insured Value

Silver

Description of Article and Location	Purchase Date	Original Price	Insured Value

HOUSEHOLD INVENTORY

Appliances

Article	Serial No.	Manufacturer	Purchase Price	Purchase Date	Warranty Period

HOUSEHOLD INVENTORY

Appliances

Article	Serial No.	Manufacturer	Purchase Price	Purchase Date	Warranty Period

HOUSEHOLD INVENTORY

Valuable Books

Description of Article and Location	Purchase Date	Original Price	Insured Value

HOUSEHOLD INVENTORY

Musical Instruments

Description of Article and Location	Purchase Date	Original Price	Insured Value

Photographic Equipment

Description of Article and Location	Purchase Date	Original Price	Insured Value

HOUSEHOLD INVENTORY

Coins

Description of Article and Location	Purchase Date	Original Price	Insured Value

HOUSEHOLD INVENTORY

Stamps

Description of Article and Location	Purchase Date	Original Price	Insured Value

HOUSEHOLD INVENTORY

Jewelry

Description of Article and Location	Purchase Date	Original Price	Insured Value

Furs

Description of Article and Location	Purchase Date	Original Price	Insured Value

HOUSEHOLD INVENTORY

Property Not Listed Elsewhere

Description of Article and Location	Purchase Date	Original Price	Insured Value

HOUSEHOLD INVENTORY

Property Not Listed Elsewhere

Description of Article and Location	Purchase Date	Original Price	Insured Value

HOUSEHOLD INVENTORY

Property Not Listed Elsewhere

Description of Article and Location	Purchase Date	Original Price	Insured Value

HOUSEHOLD INVENTORY

Summary of Household Inventory

	Original Price	Insured Value
Entrance Hall		
Den/Family Room		
Library		
Living Room		
Dining Room		
Kitchen/Breakfast Area		
Bedroom 1		
Bedroom 2		
Bedroom 3		
Bedroom 4		
Bathroom 1		
Bathroom 2		
Bathroom 3		
Linen and Storage Closets		
Utility Room		
Attic		
Basement		
Garage		

HOUSEHOLD INVENTORY

Summary of Household Inventory

	Original Price	Insured Value
Appliances		
China		
Silver		
Valuable Books		
Musical Instruments		
Photographic Equipment		
Coins		
Stamps		
Jewelry		
Furs		
Property Not Listed Elsewhere		